# EXTREME CAREERS™

# BIOHAZARD TECHNICIANS

## Life on a Trauma Scene Cleanup Crew

Stephanie Cooperman

rosen central™

The Rosen Publishing Group, Inc., New York

Published in 2004 by The Rosen Publishing Group, Inc.
29 East 21st Street, New York, NY  10010

**Library of Congress Cataloging-in-Publication Data**

Cooperman, Stephanie
Biohazard technicians: life on a trauma scene cleanup crew / by Stephanie Cooperman.
    p.  cm. — (Extreme careers)
Includes bibliographical references and index.
ISBN 0-8239-3964-2
1. Infectious wastes—Juvenile literature  2. Traumatology—Waste disposal—Vocational guidance—Juvenile literature  3. Emergency medical technicians—Vocational guidance—Juvenile literature  4. Crime scenes—Health aspects—Juvenile literature  5. Cleaning personnel—Vocational guidance—Juvenile literature
[1. Infectious wastes  2. Traumatology—Waste disposal—Vocational guidance
3. Emergency medical technicians—Vocational guidance  4. Crime scenes—Health aspects  5. Cleaning personnel—Vocational guidance
6. Vocational guidance]
I. Title II. Series
RA567.7.C66 2003
363.72'88—dc21

                                              2002-153683

*Manufactured in the United States of America*

# Contents

# Introduction Cleanup Time!

**N**eal Smither knew he wanted to be a biohazard technician after he saw the 1994 Oscar-winning movie, *Pulp Fiction*. In the film, the two lead characters accidentally shoot a passenger in the backseat of their car. Most moviegoers were shocked at the scene. But Smither was wondering who was going to clean up the blood and brains.

Like most people, Smither was not aware that businesses exist to clean up trauma scenes. They do, and biohazard technicians have the experience to deal with all kinds of blood and gore at any trauma scene. A trauma scene is any crime scene or other location where a person has suffered severe wounds caused by sudden physical injuries. Common causes

In Quentin Tarantino's 1994 film Pulp Fiction, the hitmen played by John Travolta (left) and Samuel Jackson have to deal with the bloody trauma of an accidental killing. Normally, biohazard technicians are the ones called upon in such a case.

of trauma include natural death, murder, suicide, and extreme violence.

Family members whose loved ones are victims of trauma must deal with many things. It can be an emotional time with many heavy burdens. Most people think that the police officers, firefighters, or emergency workers who respond to a trauma scene are responsible for cleaning it up. What they do not realize is that often family members are left to clean up the mess.

# Biohazard Technicians: Life on a Trauma Scene Cleanup Crew

When trauma occurs, blood, brain matter, skin particles, organs, and the urine and feces that are released when someone dies may stain carpets, walls, and furniture. If the person who died or was injured carried a disease, his or her blood may still be able to cause infection. Therefore, not everyone who attempts to clean up a trauma scene has the proper

This crime scene photo shows the blood found by police after Nicole Brown Simpson's murder. Her ex-husband, O. J. Simpson, was tried (and later aquitted) for the crime. Biohazard technicians are charged with safely cleaning up and disposing of human remains.

knowledge to avoid getting sick. Since biohazard technicians remove, package, and dispose of blood, bodily fluids, and other materials, mostly from homes after people die, they must have special training.

More important, biohazard technicians must be sensitive to the families' emotions. Trauma causes people to feel many different things—shock, anger, frustration, and sadness, to name a few. Many biohazard technicians were once police officers or emergency medical technicians. They are accustomed to seeing bloody messes at trauma scenes. They also have experience talking to family members who do not know how to deal with personal disasters. Some biohazard technicians have training as priests, ministers, or rabbis. This array of backgrounds helps them deal with delicate situations and serve as impromptu counselors for people in need.

A mere twenty years ago, trauma scene cleanup did not exist. Family members did all the work themselves—and sometimes not very successfully. Beginning in the 1980s, companies with names such as Blood Busters, Crime Scene Cleaners, and BioCare began to pop up around the country as qualified technicians soon learned there was a need for trauma cleanup services. Now there are more than five hundred biohazard removal and cleaning companies in the United States. Dressed in special protective gear—including bodysuits, gloves, boots, face shields, hoods, and respirators—the biohazard technician looks like a cross between a human marshmallow and an astronaut. Underneath the layers is an intelligent, dedicated professional trained to clean up even the worst disasters.

# Blood, Brains, and Bugs 1

**B**iohazard technicians see it all. As Neal Smither, owner of Crime Scene Cleaners, says, "Humans are animals. We're violent and we're smart." The most common trauma scene occurs with a decaying body that is not discovered for a few days because the person lived alone.

Other trauma scenes are also crime scenes, where murders, brutal fights, or suicides have taken place. Still other cleanup areas do not involve blood at all. Some people neglect their homes so badly that smelly, moldy trash is left in a room for months. Soon rats and maggots start to devour the trash.

During floods or other disasters, sewage lines can back up into people's homes. The homeowners may not know that this presents a biohazard problem. After the floodwaters recede, human urine and feces remain and can cover a room. Technicians must wade through the mess with their boots on to start scooping up what should have remained in the sewer.

The worst task that Susan Andrews of Blood Busters, in Sarasota, Florida, had to do was empty the contents of a smelly refrigerator two months after the power went off in an unoccupied home.

Sewage from overflowing sewer systems may need professional cleanup assistance. Here, a Cedar Rapids, Iowa, resident removes debris from his flooded garage after floods hit several Midwestern cities in June 2002.

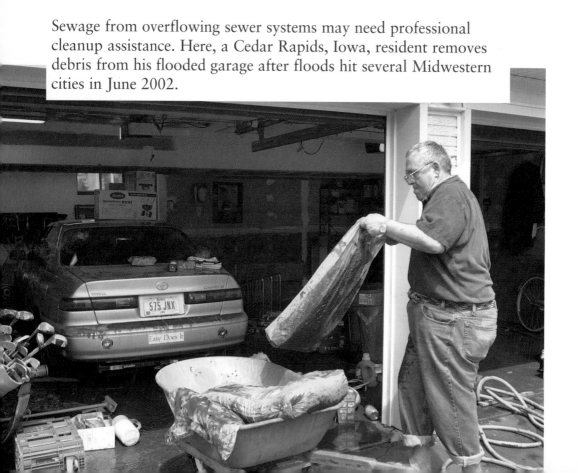

# On the Job With . . .

## Neal Smither

Biohazard technician Neal Smither knows that some trauma scenes can be harder to clean than others. He once cleaned a suicide scene three months after it occurred. A man broke into his ex-wife's house and killed himself in her bed. The woman worked in another country at the time and was gone for half the year. She did not return and find the mess until rats had eaten the entire body. Dead flies were everywhere. Smither said the floor was covered nearly a foot deep with rat feces. There were not many human remains left to dispose of because the body was completely decomposed. Only the imprint of the man's body on the bed was visible. Smither and his team had to concentrate on shoveling away the dead insects and rat droppings and hauling away the contaminated furniture.

"There are definitely jobs that wear on you," he said when recalling the incident for the book, *Gig*.

She couldn't decide which was more disgusting: the Chinese food containers that overflowed with mold or the curdled milk.

# Anything and Everything

The causes of trauma scenes vary. So does the nature of the scenes. Technicians cannot have any expectations. They must be prepared for anything.

Usually, technicians can expect to find blood or other bodily fluids. "There's a joke in the industry that blood defies all laws of physics," Kent Berg, a biohazard technician, told the *Des Moines Register*. "We find blood in places that we can't figure out how it gets there. We have to get every near-microscopic blood spot up so the family doesn't find it." Most technicians learn early that blood can be found anywhere, including in between carpet fibers and floor tiles, deep into layers of a wall, inside the cracks of windowpanes, and ingrained into wooden furniture.

# Stories of the Job

Each biohazard technician has a story about a trauma scene that sticks out in his or her mind. Some speak of the especially strong odors of decaying bodies, burnt hair, rotting food or trash, or animal feces. Susan Andrews was caught off guard by the large number of insects that once invaded a scene. She walked into a room where there had been a natural death and was met with a swarm of at least one hundred buzzing black flies that were dining on the dead body.

# Ready, Set, Clean!

**2**

Being a biohazard technician means more than showing up at a client's home or office with a bucket and a scrub brush. Technicians must protect themselves against diseases and odors that may linger after a death. They wear special clothing and safety equipment, from bodysuits to gloves to breathing masks. No technician would greet a scene dressed in a suit and tie.

## Class III Biohazard Containment Suit

The class III biohazard containment suit is a big white bodysuit that protects technicians from cuts, scrapes, or infection. The Kimberly Clark or Tyvex

Biocontainment suits are a crucial tool in keeping biohazard technicians safe from infection and other dangers. Michael and Christopher Hosto, brothers and owners of Crime Scene Cleanup, based in Fort Lauderdale, Florida, are pictured here in full gear.

companies make these patented-material suits. The material forms a protective barrier against blood and other fluids, keeping away from the skin any airborne diseases, molds, and other harmful substances.

Wearing these suits in the summer can become very hot for technicians. At these times, technicians can wear cool vests which hold ice packs on the chest to fight the heat.

## Acetate Splashguard

Just like what doctors wear in surgical rooms, the acetate splashguard is a special shield that keeps liquids off a technician's face.

## Respirator

Technicians wear full-face or half-face respirators to help them breathe. Respirators protect them from airborne diseases they might breathe in by pushing the air through a filter. The pathogens and dirt are caught in the filter and do not enter the technician's lungs.

# Vapor Lock

Dead bodies start to decay immediately and leave foul-smelling odors. Many respirators use vapor lock so that technicians won't smell the odors while they work. Vapor lock is a filtration system that attaches to the respirator. Disgusting odors like decaying skin or feces are caught in the vapor lock by a substance such as charcoal before they can enter a technician's nose.

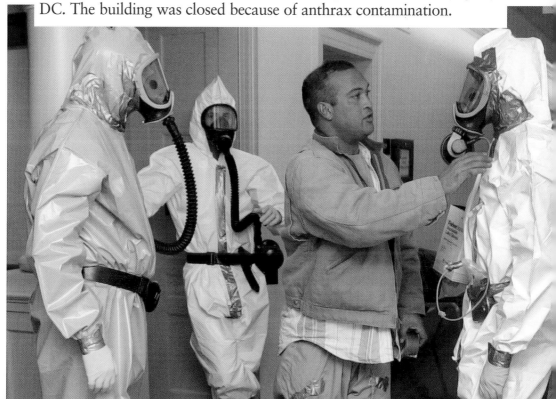

Workers gear up before entering the office of U.S. Representative Rush Holt in the Longworth House Building on Capitol Hill, in Washington, DC. The building was closed because of anthrax contamination.

# Gloves, Boots, and Hoods

Technicians wear two pairs of gloves. The first pair is made of latex—the type doctors wear—to keep out germs and dirt. Latex gloves are not very sturdy, however, so technicians also wear heavy utility gloves made of leather and spandex. The leather protects against sharp objects. The spandex stretches over the wrists and bodysuit cuffs to form a seal against fluids, dirt, and mold. Sometimes, duct tape is applied around the cuff to strengthen the seal.

The containment suits come with a hood and booties attached. Sometimes, technicians need additional heavy rubber boots when they are going into a room covered in water or sewage. The gloves, boots, and hoods are all disposable so that dirt and germs are not transferred to the next cleanup scene.

# Getting the Call

When families undergo a traumatic situation, they must think quickly. They have recently lost a loved one, and there is a mess to clean up. Since biohazard technicians usually work for private companies, it is unfair for emergency workers or police officers to recommend one over the other. They do, however, tell people that trauma scene cleaners exist. Often, and under such terrible conditions, people simply do not know about them.

Neal Smither's Crime Scene Cleaners is a national company that receives three thousand cleanup calls every year. Other companies agree that there is a huge need for their services—and quickly. "It's the kind of job where they want you there yesterday," Susan Andrews says.

Family members cannot make the call to a bio-hazard technician, however, until police "release the scene." Police officers must complete their investigation and any bodies must be removed before people can enter the crime area without disturbing the scene. In a natural death, this process takes only a day or two. But when a crime such as murder has occurred, the police must conduct a careful investigation that can take weeks. After such delays, technicians must scrub harder because substances such as blood and brain matter will have dried into carpets and onto walls.

# Cleanup Time!

Many biohazard technicians arrive at the scene in special trucks. These trucks or trailers are equipped with everything a technician needs on the job. They carry all the cleaning supplies, brushes, carpet-removal devices, deodorizer, and biohazard buckets necessary to turn a trauma scene back into a normal home or office. Technicians do not use the same everyday sponges and cleaning pads you find in local stores. They usually buy their supplies from the same companies that sell to hospitals or school cafeterias. Cleaning swabs are made of an absorbent material with a waterproof backing. That way, technicians ensure that their cleaners can absorb all the fluids and sanitize a trauma scene. The chemicals in their cleaning supplies are similar to bleach. However, bleach eats away at materials. The cleaning fluids that biohazard technicians use are equally strong, but they do not leave holes in carpets or furniture.

Biohazard technicians are more than glorified janitors. When they go into a bathroom, bedroom,

Eric Wynn, owner of a Crime Scene Cleaners franchise in Indiana, poses by one of his trucks. For $50 an hour, Wynn sells his services to families, police departments, and coroners.

hallway, or other space, their job is to leave it sparkling clean. Often this is easier said than done. When trauma occurs, blood and other bodily fluids stain carpets, floors, and furniture. Bullets can pierce walls and break glass. Chairs and tables can be overturned or broken. Damage can consume an entire house. In these cases, biohazard technicians have a huge job ahead of them. They work hard for days to remove the contaminated items from the home and to make it livable again.

# A Safe Area

When first entering a trauma scene, technicians create a safe area. This is the place where they keep their clean supplies and are able to use the bathroom. They certainly do not want to take germs in there! The safe area cannot have any contamination from the actual trauma scene.

Some technicians have trailers that are large enough to contain a safe area that is outside of and away from the trauma scene. Usually, however, the safe area is a room in the house where no trauma has occurred. Technicians put a runner—or path—between the safe area and the trauma room. The runner can be made of heavy craft paper or plastic. Technicians travel back and forth from the safe area to the trauma scene on the runner as they are working. They must make certain, however, that they change out of their protective clothing—from their hoods down to their booties— before they reenter the safe room.

Seattle-based Crime Scene Sanitation is run by husband-and-wife team Jim and Janie Liles. Their company specializes in crime scene trauma cleanup. Some jobs can be more gruesome than others, so professionals like the Lileses need strong stomachs.

# Get to It!

Technicians start the cleanup by doing what they call load reduction. This means they take away the heaviest contaminated items in the area. They lift out heavy furniture such as sofas or couches that are dripping with blood, brain matter, or decayed organs and put them in the truck. With sledgehammers, they knock down walls that are too dirty to be cleaned. They rip away carpeting and flooring with carpet cutters' carpentry tools. They even use their hands if the blood and mucus have been absorbed into the smallest carpet fibers or wooden panels, where machines cannot complete the job. It is up to the family or business owner to replace walls and flooring that need to be removed.

Once the big items are cleared, they can get busy with some of the dirtiest work. Usually, technicians use only mops when they need to clean a large area. Don McNulty owns Bio Cleaning Services, based in Kansas City, Missouri. He once cleaned a convenience store where someone had been shot and ran around the store fleeing the assailant. There were little splatters of blood up and down the aisles, and McNulty used a mop for that project.

Technicians mostly use absorbent sponges, towels, or pads to wipe up hair particles, blood, and organ remains that are too liquefied to be picked up with their hands. They dip a sponge in the strong cleaning fluid and wipe it over the flooring or walls to remove the signs of death and decay. They repeat this process many times over until they have removed all the blood, fluids, and body pieces they can find.

There are limits to how clean technicians can make an area. Their cleaning products kill any disease that still lives. "But the area cannot be sterilized," Susan Andrews says. "It is sanitized. That means it's 95 percent clear of all bacteria and viruses." After they remove soiled furniture, pull up contaminated carpets, and disinfect the area, technicians usually need to deodorize. Trauma breeds foul-smelling odors. Technicians use an ozone generator to clear the air after decomposition has occurred. Ozone, sometimes called activated oxygen, kills bacteria, viruses, and odors. It contains three atoms of oxygen instead of the two atoms found in the oxygen we breathe from the air. This structure allows ozone to kill bacteria by breaking their cell walls. When the bacteria are destroyed, so is the smell.

# Stop in the Name of the Law!

When biohazard technicians clean up violent crime scenes—where murders or brutal fights have occurred—they must be especially careful. While cleaning crime scenes, technicians can find items that may be helpful to the police in their investigation. The police comb a scene to find clues as to who committed the crime. But they may miss an object that is covered with blood or other bodily fluids. Technicians may find bullet shell casings, human hairs, or pieces of torn clothing that may lead authorities to the criminal.

Keith Brown once found part of a bullet that helped the police in their investigation. He did what all biohazard technicians are supposed to do when they find an object that might be considered evidence. "We immediately stopped working and called the police," he says. "That way, they could come pick up the item before we proceeded."

It is important that technicians do not talk about their work with people outside their company. Everything they see remains confidential. This rule protects the family's privacy and makes sure the public won't interfere with police work.

Technicians work closely with the police. Police Chief Dan Lawrence of Orinda, California, told the *Contra Costa Times* that "in the old days, we'd have an orderly get in there and clean blood from a cell or a squad car. Now we recognize the need for being prepared to safely remove biohazards." Sometimes, technicians also help out the police department in their area. They may clean police cars or jail cells free of charge. Some even clean blood-stained police uniforms to help out their local force.

# Removing Waste

Once cleaning materials are soiled with the soupy mess, they cannot be used again. Anything stained with blood or bodily fluids must be put in a biohazard bag or plastic barrel. Most people have seen the

Investigators survey biohazard collection containers near the crash site of US Airways flight 427. The airliner crashed in the Pennsylvania countryside on September 11, 2001, after passengers attempted to overwhelm the hijackers who had taken over the plane.

biohazard sign; it is the fluorescent orange or orange red four-circle symbol that is commonly seen in doctors' offices or hospitals. The receptacles that technicians fill must have this symbol on them or be colored red. It does not matter whether they are from a home improvement store or a waste disposal company, as long as the three circles are there. Although the materials that technicians put in biohazard containers might not cause disease, technicians must act as if everything they come into contact with can cause illness.

Once all the materials contaminated by blood or other bodily fluids have been put in the special biohazard bags or containers, technicians can load up their trucks. Where do all the hazardous materials go? Not to a regular trash compactor or landfill, that's for certain. Biohazardous materials must be taken to a special place so that they do not harm other people. Most often, tech-

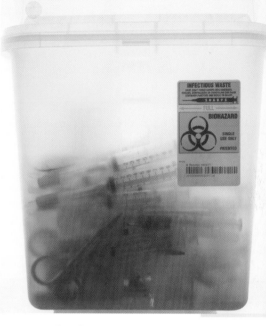

This is a medical waste container, just like the ones doctors use. The prominent biohazard symbol warns others that the contents can be dangerous.

nicians take their full bags or canisters to biohazardous waste incinerators or reduction centers run by the city or state. At the incinerator, the soiled furniture, carpets, or other materials are burned or ground into mulch in a safe environment that kills all remaining pathogens. If

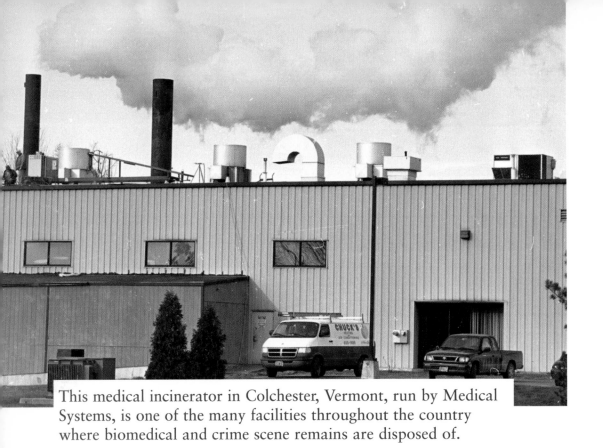

This medical incinerator in Colchester, Vermont, run by Medical Systems, is one of the many facilities throughout the country where biomedical and crime scene remains are disposed of.

the technicians hand in used canisters, they are given new clean ones.

Technicians can get rid of the waste another way. They can also suck up all the blood and bodily fluids with a machine called an extractor. An extractor is like a special wet/dry vacuum. The hazardous waste is slurped into a tank. There, an enzyme hits it and kills any bacteria or viruses that may still be alive. The enzyme takes all the dangerous materials out of the waste. It no longer needs to be taken to an incinerator. It can even be flushed down the toilet! The contaminated furniture and carpets are then taken to a garbage dump or landfill.

# No Guts, No Glory

Most technicians enter the biohazard cleanup business almost by accident. In one case, a couple of technicians ran a carpet-cleaning business that one day received a frantic call from a customer who couldn't get blood out of his carpet. Susan Andrews and her partner, Brenda Bernius, both had relatives die at home. They started Blood Busters when they realized there was no one to call to clean up the bodily fluids after the bodies had been taken away.

For Don McNulty of Bio Cleaning Services, it was a call from a desperate man who showed him that biohazard cleanup was a good business risk. "His sixteen-year-old boy had committed suicide," McNulty says. "He said I was the twelfth person he called. He said if I couldn't help him, who could?" McNulty decided he needed to help.

However, many new technicians fail because they do not realize what to expect. It is not easy money, and it is not for thrill seekers. "You have to have a special mind-set to do this day in and day out," another biohazard technician, Kent Berg, told the *Des Moines Register*. Biohazard technicians must want to help people. They must come prepared with an attention to detail and a willingness to deal with horrible scenes.

# Tough Minds and Bodies

Keith Brown was a police officer in Cedar Rapids, Iowa, for ten years before he became a biohazard technician. He saw his fair share of stabbings, shootings, and other deaths. When he started a carpet-cleaning company, he had no idea that his ability to clean up trauma scenes would be so profitable. Brown heard about the need for trauma scene cleaners from people who were already in the business.

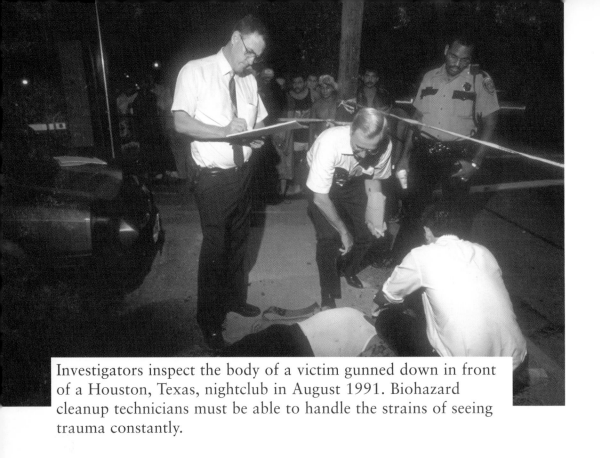

Investigators inspect the body of a victim gunned down in front of a Houston, Texas, nightclub in August 1991. Biohazard cleanup technicians must be able to handle the strains of seeing trauma constantly.

He did his own research to find out how to become a biohazard technician. He was not squeamish about blood or dead bodies because of his time on the force. He thought he could handle the pressures of biohazard cleanup. So, less than two years later, he turned in his badge to concentrate on his business full-time.

Brown is like many other technicians across the country. They knew they could help families in need—families who have enough to handle without the added burden of cleaning up a trauma scene. And they knew they could make money doing it.

"I don't know how the cops do it," Neal Smither told the *Contra Costa Times*. "It's disgusting, but it keeps me in business. I love this job, and I'll probably always be in it."

# A Clean Shoulder to Lean On

After a biohazard technician receives a call from a family in need, he or she makes an appointment to come to the trauma scene. Technicians must bring all their protective gear with them. Some families are not happy about this. According to Keith Brown, some people become nervous when they see the large white suits and respirators being put on. According to Brown, "They will say 'What will the neighbors think?' but we have to protect ourselves."

"Sensitivity is the key," Susan Andrews says. "The family is going through a very difficult time, and we don't want to add to their grief." Family members explain to the technicians what they can expect when they enter the scene. Technicians then tell the

# On the Job With . . .

## Don McNulty

Technician Don McNulty always has his crew act in a professional manner at a trauma scene. They never tell jokes or laugh. They do not play the radio. According to McNulty, technicians must act like funeral directors. The family has been through a troubling event. The technicians must show respect at all times. They realize that they are much more than typical cleaners. "Care, concern, and peace of mind" is the motto of McNulty's company. "That's what we sell," he says.

family what items need to be removed and what items they can sanitize to make the area clean and disease-free. They answer the family's questions. For example, they might say that they can knock down a wall with bullet holes, remove the bed where the victim was shot, and clean the hardwood floor that is contaminated with blood and brain matter, but they cannot replace a shattered window.

# It's a Hard-Knock Life

Being a biohazard technician is often a grueling job. They must see the aftermath of trauma firsthand. They must deal with a grieving family. And when they go home at night, they know they must do it again the next day.

The emotional effects of this kind of work are very real. It takes a mentally tough person to do the job. Technicians not only do physical labor, but they must also face gruesome sights. Blood and bodily fluids are a daily part of the job.

Don McNulty has seen his fair share of trauma scenes. Based in the cattle country of Missouri, he lives in an area where people love to eat meat. But to this day he cannot eat a rare steak because it reminds him too much of the blood he sees. Keith Brown can deal with the blood; however, his wife—who also works as a technician—is a bit squeamish around blood. Susan Andrews does not think her job is for the weak. "No one should see what I've seen," she said.

Yet, some technicians may be in for more than a feeling of shock when they see an especially bad trauma scene. What they have seen can haunt them even after they take the last biohazard bag to the local incinerator. Some technicians have nightmares or trouble sleeping.

# Critical Incident Stress Syndrome

Some biohazard technicians suffer from critical incident stress syndrome, a condition people suffer when they witness a particularly horrifying event. They are often haunted by flashbacks of the scene or refuse to go anywhere that reminds them of what they saw. The severity of this syndrome depends on the person, of course.

However, biohazard technicians undergo a great deal of emotional stress when they clean up a trauma scene. That is why there is such a high turnover rate in the business. Technicians who cannot deal with the stress often quit early on. Many technicians feel this stress even when their telephones ring. On the one hand, they are excited about the new business opportunity. On the other, they are anxious about what awaits them at the trauma scene.

Therefore, biohazard technicians must protect their minds as much as they protect their bodies. It is good for them to talk to each other about what they

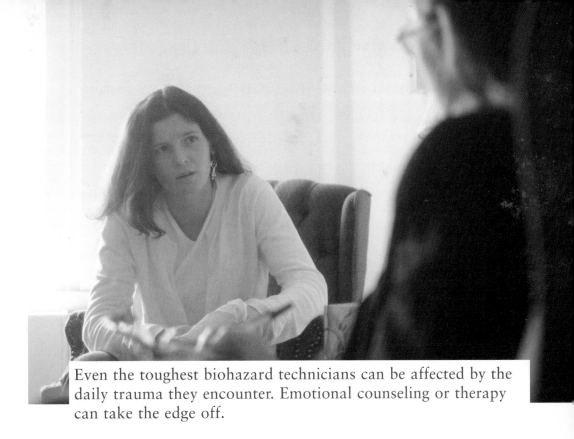

Even the toughest biohazard technicians can be affected by the daily trauma they encounter. Emotional counseling or therapy can take the edge off.

have seen. Sometimes, they also speak to counselors who deal with death. Many technicians work with family members. That way they can deal with the trauma together.

# Helping Families to Cope

Biohazard technicians usually do not have training in dealing with distraught family members. Technically, that is not part of the job. However, many family members try to discuss the trauma with technicians before or after they do the cleaning. Working at a trauma scene is a very personal job. Many families feel a connection with the people who are cleaning up the mess.

Some technicians feel that they can help these families. They bring books about grieving to their clients. Others are former police officers or emergency medical technicians. They are accustomed to seeing the blood and gore that goes along with the job. They can comfort families by being calm and rational even when they are seeing something gruesome. Keith Brown, a former police officer, agrees. "You learn to tune out what you're seeing," he told the *Des Moines Register.* Some technicians even have a religious background. They were once pastors, ministers, priests, or rabbis. They know how to deal with death from the point of view of a particular religion.

# Tricks of the Trade

4

**N**eal Smither's truck is easy to remember. It has special "DOA CLNR" license plates. His company's name and its slogan are painted on the door: Crime Scene Cleaners, Inc. Homicides, Suicides and Accidental Deaths. No one forgets Susan Andrews's company shirt with its bright Blood Busters logo, either.

## The Rules of the Game

Catchy slogans and fancy trucks are not all a person needs to become a biohazard technician. Handling dangerous substances requires specialized training.

Rescue workers evacuate a "victim" while training in downtown Richmond, Virginia. Emergency teams had to respond to a simulated bioterrorist attack.

The U.S. Department of Labor has a division called the Occupational Safety and Health Administration (OSHA). OSHA has created regulations 1910.1030 for dealing with bloodborne pathogens or diseases that may linger in blood after it leaves the body (such as hepatitis, tuberculosis, and HIV, or human immunodeficiency virus—the virus that causes AIDS).

OSHA's rules require each company to have a written exposure control plan. This plan outlines how the company is going to protect its employees against harmful contamination and what to do if a technician becomes infected. OSHA also has regulations to help implement the plan, including suggestions for protective clothing and methods for disposing of hazardous waste. Every year biohazard technicians must be retrained in the bloodborne pathogen exposure control plan. OSHA might change the rules slightly each year. It might add or delete regulations based on new findings about diseases that can live in blood. Technicians must know about these changes every year. They must also get shots to protect against hepatitis B. Even though many of the trauma scenes a technician cleans may be disease-free, he or she must act as if there is always a chance for infection.

# Teaching Others

Don McNulty recognized that people who wanted to enter the business had nowhere to turn for advice and help. McNulty began to teach a two-day course on how to clean up a trauma scene—no matter what technicians encounter. "It's a basic biotechnician course," McNulty says. Blood, brain matter, and skin particles can wind up in diverse places such as the cushions of a sofa or between floor tiles. McNulty helps new technicians learn to do battle with all the demons of decay.

It is impossible to exactly re-create traumatic events, and it is impossible to plan for death. Therefore, McNulty and his team use cow blood and pig brains to make the scene look real. No one sits by idly in this course! Participants take turns wearing the required protective gear and cleaning up the mess using the special cleaners, sponges, and containers. Others watch and learn how it is done through example.

# The American Bio-Recovery Association

McNulty's course is not the only place where technicians can go for training. Although there are no actual biohazard schools, other courses are popping up around the country. The American Bio-Recovery Association (ABRA) is a nonprofit association of crime and trauma scene recovery professionals that also trains and certifies aspiring biohazard technicians.

In order to become a member of ABRA, a technician's company must fulfill certain requirements. He or she has to be in business for at least six months. He or she must know how to deal with bloodborne pathogens, respiratory protection, and other possible contaminants while on the job, and must have insurance. Finally, a small annual fee is required. Once a member in ABRA, companies have the benefit of talking about their work and getting ideas from other biohazard technicians. They can also attend annual conferences on the industry and receive additional hands-on training.

Since no training other than that of OSHA is required, training differs from state to state. Most courses use simulations. There, students watch a teacher scrubbing away fake human blood with sponges, scooping up fake decayed skin and bones with absorbent pads, and removing the fake human remains in biohazard bags and containers. By seeing an expert clean a simulated infected area, students learn the two most important things for biohazard cleanup: how to clear away all blood, guts, and dirt so that the scene looks clean and how to get rid of all possible pathogens so that the scene is clean.

Aspiring technicians are not required to go to cleanup classes. They can also buy how-to books on the Internet or through specialty bookstores on cleaning up trauma scenes. Both how-to courses and books teach technicians about national regulations.

Technicians also need to know other things, such as regulations specific to the area they work in and how to run a successful business. However, would-be technicians must find this information on their own. They can call municipal offices in their area or enroll in business classes.

# Other Biological Hazards 5

As Neal Smither told the *Contra Costa Times*, "Gore sells, and there's no way to sugarcoat it." Gore is also expensive to clean up. This means good profits for the biohazard cleanup business.

An average trauma scene cleanup takes two to five hours and costs between a few hundred dollars and more than $3,000. The amount of time it takes and the price it costs depends largely on the size of the job and how long the blood and other bodily fluids have been there. Most cleanup jobs are covered by the home-owner's insurance. This makes it easier for the family. They don't need to quibble about money when they know the cost of the cleanup is being taken care of.

Naturally occurring environmental hazards, such as the black mold pictured here, can plague unsuspecting homeowners. This mold was found in a house on the Turtle Mountain Indian Reservation in Belcourt, North Dakota.

# Added Services

As the need for biohazard technicians expands, so do the types of services they offer. Large companies now have contracts with national stores. They are the only technicians that can be called when a trauma occurs in one of the chain's stores. Some technicians not only clean a trauma scene but also make the room look exactly the way it did before the incident. This may include replacing furniture or rebuilding walls.

Other technicians remove black mold, or *Stachybotrys chartarum*—a substance that can make people very sick with headaches, rashes, or memory loss, and can even cause death. Like the mold found on bread left in the refrigerator too long, black mold is attracted to moisture, darkness, and warm temperatures. This makes the insulation in

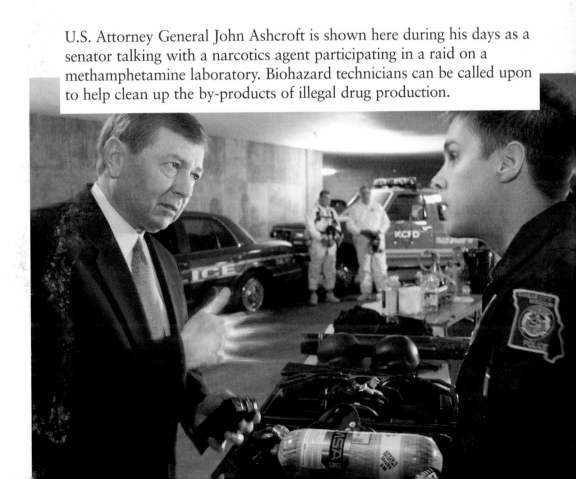

U.S. Attorney General John Ashcroft is shown here during his days as a senator talking with a narcotics agent participating in a raid on a methamphetamine laboratory. Biohazard technicians can be called upon to help clean up the by-products of illegal drug production.

walls and certain wallpapers the ideal place for black mold to fester and begin destroying a building.

Other technicians clean up methamphetamine labs. In a meth lab, people illegally produce the drug methamphetamine. Making the drug produces lots of toxic waste. Walls can become yellow with residue. Floors are usually covered with red phosphorus. Technicians clean a meth lab by using the same precautions and materials they would use to remove a dead body.

# Fighting Bioterrorism

In autumn 2001, terrorists tried to spread the disease anthrax. They sent letters containing a white powder to major corporations and government offices throughout the United States. The powder contained a strain of the anthrax disease, which sometimes proved to be fatal. Biohazard technicians were the perfect people for the cleanup jobs required by these incidents. Government officials and businesses contacted biohazard technicians

Biohazard workers enter the Hart Senate Office Building in Washington, DC, on November 6, 2001, at the height of the anthrax scare, when spores were found in the building.

to clean areas where anthrax contamination may have occurred.

As more people become experienced biohazard technicians, the job description will continue to change. There is an inexhaustible market for their work. People will continue to die—sometimes in very violent ways. Family members count on the technicians' expertise to remove soiled items and to protect them from disease. Like the anthrax cases, there will also be a need for technicians to clean up hazardous substances that could never be expected.

As the competition grows, technicians will be forced to train better and work harder. Most technicians are already marketing their companies to their service areas. Some technicians work in only one city, while others are trying to cover the entire country. Crime Scene Cleaners already has offices in seventeen states and employees in nearly all the rest. "We will be the McDonald's of blood," Neal Smither says, referring to how large he wants his company's franchise operation to grow. Whether they work for small or large companies, biohazard technicians have a valuable job to do.

# So, You Want to Be a Biohazard Technician?

So you think you can handle this extreme career? You aren't grossed out by blood, guts, or a decaying body or two? Biohazard cleanup is a hot career. The industry is only going to grow in the future. Just make certain you know what you're getting yourself into. Carpets soaked in blood, walls marked by bullets, and mattresses ruined by decaying bodies are typical components of the job. Grab a containment suit, a respirator, some gloves, and the best cleaning fluids available. There is a trauma scene to clean.

# Glossary

**biohazard containment suit**  The white bodysuit that helps technicians protect their bodies from cuts, injury, or infection.

**biohazard technician**  A person who cleans up a trauma scene.

**black mold**  A mold that lives in buildings and can make people sick.

**bloodborne pathogen**  A bacteria or virus that is spread through the blood.

**bodily fluids**  Things like blood, urine, feces, and brain matter that may remain after someone dies.

**critical incident stress syndrome**  An emotional condition similar to posttraumatic stress disorder that technicians can suffer after cleaning a trauma scene.

**extractor** A machine that kills the bacteria in bodily fluids with a special enzyme.

**incinerator** The facility that burns waste materials.

**load reduction** The method technicians use to clean by removing the heaviest part of the contamination first.

**OSHA** The Occupational Safety and Health Administration, which has regulations for handling bloodborne pathogens.

**ozone** A gas made of three oxygen atoms that kills bacteria and odors.

**respirator** A device that protects technicians from airborne diseases by filtering air.

**safe area** The place where technicians keep their clean supplies and travel to the bathroom.

**trauma scene** Any area, room, or building where a body has been discovered after death by natural causes or sudden physical injuries, such as from a murder or suicide.

**vapor lock** A filtration system that attaches to a technician's respirator and blocks foul odors.

# For More Information

## Organizations

American Bio-Recovery Association (ABRA)
P.O. Box 828
Ipswich, MA 01938
(888) 979-2272
Web site: http://www.americanbiorecovery.org

Occupational Safety and Health Administration
U.S. Department of Labor
200 Constitution Avenue NW
Washington, DC 20210
(202) 693-2000
Web site: http://www.osha.gov

# Web Sites

Due to the changing nature of Internet links, the Rosen Publishing Group, Inc., has developed an online list of Web sites related to the subject of this book. This site is updated regularly. Please use this link to access the list:

http://www.rosenlinks.com/ec/bite/

# For Further Reading

Bowe, John, Marisa Bowe, and Sabin Streeter, eds.
    *Gig: Americans Talk About Their Jobs.* New York:
    Three Rivers Press, 2001.

Brookesmith, Peter, et al., eds. *Biohazard: The Hot
    Zone and Beyond.* New York: Barnes and Noble
    Books, 1997.

Cohen, Gary, and John O'Connor, eds. *Fighting
    Toxics: A Manual for Protecting Your Family,
    Community and Workplace.* Washington, DC:
    Island Press, 1990.

Harris, Barbara, et al. *Crime Scene Investigation.*
    Westport, CT: Teacher Ideas Press, 1998.

Zipko, Stephen James. *Toxic Threat: How Hazardous
    Substances Poison Our Lives.* Englewood Cliffs, NJ:
    Silver Burdett Press, 1990.

# Bibliography

Andrews, Susan. Telephone interview with author, New York, NY, August 9, 2002.

"Bloodborne Pathogens." Occupational Safety and Health Administration Web site. Retrieved September 10, 2002 (http://www.osha.gov/SLTC/bloodbornepathogens/index.html).

Bowe, John, Marisa Bowe, and Sabin Streeter, eds. *Gig: Americans Talk About Their Jobs*. New York: Three Rivers Press, 2001.

Brown, Keith. Telephone interview with author, New York, NY, August 8, 2002.

Ford, George C. "Couple's Company Cleans Up After a Crime or Trauma," The Associated Press, June 3, 2002.

Jones, David S. "Black Mold: Between Hype and Hysteria." Real Estate Center at Texas A&M University. Retrieved September 15, 2002 (http://recenter.tamu.edu/news/4-0901.html).

McNulty, Don. Telephone interview with author, New York, NY, August 9, 2002, and September 17, 2002.

Miille, Anne. "Making a Business of Bloodstains," *Sarasota (Florida) Herald-Tribune*, May 13, 2002.

Ramsland, Katherine. The Crime Library. "Henry C. Lee Interview." Retrieved August 2, 2002 (http://www.crimelibrary.com/forensics/henry_lee/index.htm).

Ramzy, Austin. "Businesses Specialize in Cleanup of Bodies," *Des Moines Register*, July 9, 2002.

Runolfson, Mary. "Entrepreneur Goes Where Others Wince to Tread," *Contra Costa (California) Times*, July 25, 2002.

Smither, Neal. Telephone interview with author, New York, NY, August 5, 2002.

"What Is Ozone?" Air-Zone Ozone Generators Web Site. Retrieved September 15, 2002 (http://www.air-zone.com/whatisozone.html).

# Index

# About the Author

Stephanie Cooperman, a graduate of the University of Pennsylvania, is currently employed at a large book publishing company. She is a writer who freelances for print and Web site materials. She has enormous respect for biohazard technicians—both for their hard work and strong stomachs. The author of *Extreme Sports: Wakeboarding* and *Chien-Shiung Wu*, Cooperman lives in New York City.

# Photo Credits

Cover © Reuters NewMedia/Corbis ; p. 5 © The Everett Collection; pp. 6, 10, 15, 17, 21, 23, 28, 30, 42, 48, 49 © AP/Wide World Photos; p. 29 © ER Productions/Corbis; p. 34 © Shelly Katz/Timepix; p. 39 © Tom Stewart/Corbis; p. 51 © Win McNamee/Reuters/Corbis.